BYGONE FALMOUTH

Bygone Falmouth

Sheila Bird

Phillimore

1985

Published by
PHILLIMORE & CO. LTD.,
Shopwyke Hall, Chichester, Sussex

ISBN 0 85033 571 X

Printed and bound in Great Britain by
BILLING & SONS LIMITED
Worcester, England

To
Falmouth folk

LIST OF ILLUSTRATIONS

The Haven from Three Points of View
1. The Haven and Falmouth from St
   Mawes, c. 1800
2. Falmouth town, c. 1800
3. South-easterly aspect of the Haven, 1831

Early Days
4. Killigrew Memorial, Budock, 1567
5. Killigrew Monument, Grove Place
   c. 1900
6. Arwenack Manor
7. Pendennis Castle
8. Pendennis cannon
9. Sir Walter Raleigh, c. 1580
10. Facsimile of warrant to execute
    Charles I, 1648
11. Charles I window, parish church
12. Barquentine *Mozart*
13. Marlborough House
14. Tide Mill, Bar Pool, c. 1885

Views
15. Bathing beach, Gyllyngvase, c. 1865
16. Falmouth and the Penryn river
17. Railway, docks and town, c. 1900
18. Flushing from Greenbank, c. 1900
19. St Anthony lighthouse, c. 1900
20. Coastline westwards from Pendennis,
    1901
21. Falmouth town, 1901
22. Jacob's Ladder, c. 1903
23. Arwenack Avenue, c. 1903
24. Greenbank from Flushing
25. View towards Pennance Point, June
    1912
26. Pendennis from Marine Drive
27. Custom House Basin, 1912
28. The Retreat, Swanpool
29. Lead mine, Swanpool, c. 1860
30. Swanpool lead mine and waste tip,
    c. 1910
31. Feeding swans, Swanpool, c. 1890

Street Scenes
32. Lower Killigrew Street, c. 1880
33. Market stalls, The Moor, 1890
34. Tête à tête, Falmouth station c. 1900
35. Custom House c. 1900
36. Quay Hill c. 1900
37. The Old Curiosity Shop, 1910
38. High Street, c. 1900

Buildings
39. Swiss Cottage c. 1900
40. *Greenbank Hotel* c. 1904
41. High Street dwellings
42. *Falmouth Hotel*, c. 1913
43. Smithick Hill, 1936
44. Gyllyng Street, c. 1937
45. Cliff Place, 1937

Falmouth Lifeboat
46. *Jane Whittingham*, lifeboat, c. 1890
47. *Bob Newbon*, lifeboat crew, c. 1900
48. *Bob Newbon's* heroic return, 1 February
    1914
49. Launching of *Crawford & Constance
    Conybeare*, 1940
50. Arthur 'Toby' West

Falmouth Docks
51. Plan of dockyard development, c. 1855
52. Falmouth docks, 1887
53. Falmouth docks, (charcoal sketch), (1919)
54. Number 2 graving dock in course of con-
    struction, 1920
55. Aerial view of docks, 1928
56. S.S. *Strathlyon* on fire, 1908
57. Dockyard scene, 1922
58. Excavation work, c. 1940

To Falmouth for Repairs
59. S.S. *Highland Fling*, 1907
60. Ketch barge *Lady Daphne*, (sketch by
    Tony Warren), 1927

61. Crumpled bow of *Samos*

Shipping Round the Harbour
62. H.M.S. *Ganges*
63. Lads of H.M.S. *Ganges*
64. Frigate *Foudroyant*, c. 1900
65. *Victoria* and *Roseland*, about 1905
66. Flushing ferry *Express*, c. 1908
67. Tug boat *Penguin*, c. 1910
68. *Queen of the Fal*
69. Ketch barge *Eclipse*, c. 1920
70. Sailing barge *Regina*, Custom House Basin, c. 1920
71. Topsail schooner, *Mary Barrow*
72. *Foudroyant* and *Cutty Sark*, c. 1922
73. H.M.S. *Implacable*
74. Steam tug *Northgate Scott*, c. 1926
75. *Princess Maud* and *New Resolute*

Fishing
76. Fish Strand Quay, about 1890
77. Fishing fleet, 1900
78. Landing fish, c. 1900
79. Oyster dredging, Carrick Roads
80. Fishing vessels safely home, c. 1900
81. *Boy Willie*, Fish Strand Quay, c. 1920

Transport and Services
82. Errand boy and *Pamir*
83. Last mail coach leaves Falmouth, 1863
84. R.A. Militia, Pendennis, 1890
85. Belletti's horse-drawn delivery cart, c. 1895
86. First passenger car leaves Falmouth, 1904
87. Outside Prince of Wales pier, 1910
88. Laundry service vehicle, 1910
89. Falmouth policemen, 1900-13
90. Falmouth's new steam fire engine, 1910
91. Falmouth's first motor bus, 1912
92. Welcoming Falmouth's first ambulance
93. Belletti's garage
94. Railway and Progress

Recollections of War
95. First World War submarines, c. 1914
96. H.M.S. *Falmouth*
97. Warships in Falmouth Bay, c. 1914
98. British tank, The Moor, c. 1920
99. Torpedo boat, *Ardent*, being broken up
100. *St Gerrans*, c. 1938
101. Dockyard bomb damage, 1940 (painting by C. Pears)
102. Bomb damaged *British Chancellor*, July 1940
103. 'Wings for Victory' appeal, 1940
104. May morning, Falmouth 1944, (painting by Tony Warren)
105. American army landing craft, World War II
106. Aboard American army landing craft

Institutions, Events and Happenings
107. Roman Catholic church, c. 1920
108. Morgawr, monster of Falmouth Bay, (sketch by G. Vinnicombe)
109. The Bethel, sailors' rest
110. The Observatory, Western Terrace
111. Seafront chapel, c. 1900
112. Outside Ossie's shop, c. 1920
113. Fire in High Street, 1862
114. Fire in Market Street, 1870
115. Round the houses race, 1910
116. Wrecked *Bay of Panama*, 1891
117. H.M.S. *St Vincent*, Falmouth
118. Anchor of H.M.S. *St Vincent*
119. Holdroff's sail loft, c. 1900
120. Interior of Holdroff's sail loft
121. Prince of Wales foundation stone ceremony
122. Dedication of Falmouth packet obelisk, 19 November 1898
123. Proclamation of King George V, 9 May 1910
124. Plane rescue at sea
125. The King's pipe
126. Falmouth Harbour Commissioners
127. King George VI at docks, May 1942
128. Swanpool model yacht regatta, 1906
129. Quay punts, Falmouth regatta, 1895
130. *Boy Willie* cruising
131. Working boats, *Six Brothers* and *Victory*
132. Ferris built *Six Brothers*
133. 1982 Falmouth Tall Ships Race: *Gorch Fock*
134. Aboard the *Gorch Fock*
135. Polish ship, *Pogoria*
136. Brigantine *Outlaw*

People
137. Miss Anna Maria Fox
138. E. A. Osborne, Falmouth photographer
139. Henry Scott Tuke, artist
140. John West, marine artist
141. Pascoe family and friends
142. Dennis Pascoe
143. Norman Morrison with sturgeon
144. Tony Warren, marine artist
145. Young Vivian Pentecost
146. Vivian Pentecost a few years on
147. Prize winning catch
148. Tim Vinnicombe emptying a dredge

ACKNOWLEDGEMENTS

In compiling this book on Falmouth I have worked very closely with many of the townsfolk and am highly appreciative of all the encouragement, goodwill and practical help I have received. In particular I should like to mention Dennis Pascoe and Penny Maunder for a great welcome and memorable adventures around the Falmouth Docks, and Jimmy Morrison, Tony Warren, Maurice Osborne, George Vinnicombe, Vivian Pentecost and Toby West for many happy hours spent yarning in their homes, on boats, on quays and in waterside pubs, which made the preparation of this book such great fun. Thanks also to Fisher Barham, Terry Barham, Gloria Parker, Captain David Banks, Roy Stribley, Falmouth Docks, the Falmouth Packet, Falmouth Library, Falmouth Maritime Museum, the Polytechnic Society, Royal Institution of Cornwall County Museum and Art Gallery, Truro, the Local Studies Department of Redruth Library and the British Museum for all their help.

For the use of photographs I am indebted to: Peter Gilson and the Polytechnic Society for numbers 1, 2, 3, 14, 15, 17, 28, 29, 30, 34, 39, 41, 43, 45, 56, 59, 65, 66, 67, 68, 75, 78, 80, 82, 83, 85, 86, 87, 88, 90, 92, 95, 97, 98, 99, 109, 114, 121, 122 and 123; Maurice Osborne for numbers 4, 6, 10, 11, 13, 32, 33, 35, 36, 44, 46, 47, 48, 49, 63, 69, 70, 71, 73, 74, 84, 89, 96, 103, 111, 112, 113, 117, 118, 119, 120, 124, 125, 128, 129, 137, 138, 139 and 140; Falmouth Docks for numbers 51, 52, 53, 54, 55, 57, 58, 61, 101, 102; Dennis Pascoe for numbers 141 and 142; Falmouth Docks and courtesy of Colour Library International (Keystone Press Agency) for number 127; Royal Institution of Cornwall, County Museum, Truro for numbers 20, 21, 25, 26, 27, 37, 105, 106 and 110; Roy Stribley for number 100; Fisher Barham for numbers 12, 38, 62, 91, 93, 94, 115 and 116; Falmouth Maritime Museum and Fisher Barham for number 72; George Vinnicombe for numbers 81, 108, 130, 131, 132, 147 and 148; Vivian Pentecost for number 145; Tony Warren for numbers 60, 64, 76 and 104; Jimmy Morrison for numbers 79 and 143; British Library for number 9; Daphne Bryant for numbers 18, 19, 31 and 77; Captain David Banks and Falmouth Harbour Commissioners for number 126; numbers 5, 16, 22, 23, 24, 40 and 42 are from the author's own collection and numbers 7, 8, 50, 133, 134, 135, 136, 144 and 146 were taken by the author.

Last, but by no means least, I would like to thank John Miles, Maurice Osborne, David Clarke, Brian Errington, Julian Bates and the County Museum, Truro for help with high quality photographic work.

FALMOUTH

THE SALTY OLD TOWN of Falmouth, situated on the shores of one of the finest natural harbours in the world, was an insignificant little fishing settlement back in the Middle Ages when nearby Penryn was an important market centre and seat of learning and Truro was an increasingly busy port.

The haven, described by early historians as 'very notable and famous, in a manner the most principal of all Britayne' and where 'a hundred sail of vessels may anchor and not see the mast of another', was ideally positioned on trade routes for vessels needing repairs and as a place of refuge and shelter.

The area which has always been vulnerable to attacks from the sea was likely to have had a succession of fortifications on Pendennis headland long before Henry VIII ordered the construction of Pendennis Castle in 1539. Pendennis and St Mawes castles formed part of an intensive system of fortifications all along the south coast at a time when there were threats of renewed attacks from the Continent. The soldiers manning the castle suffered a cruel and deprived existence, even by standards of those days. It was fortunate for them that when the Spaniards attacked Penzance, Mousehole and Newlyn in 1595 the weather conditions were unfavourable for an attack on Pendennis, for the men were too weak to have put up much of a fight. After this the defence systems around the castle were further strengthened and adapted for use in times of war. In 1646 when the Civil War reached Cornwall, St Mawes castle swiftly fell to a landward attack and Pendennis castle, under the direction of 87-year-old Colonel John Arundell, stuck out for a siege which lasted six months.

It was the Killigrew family, who lived at Arwenack House and held the manor incorporating the land in Budock and Pendennis, who began to shape the development of the town. Sir Walter Raleigh, on visiting the place, was so struck with the area and its potential that he urged the development of a township. The economic advantages of this were attractive to Sir John Killigrew who had influence at court, and as a result of this, inns were built at Smithick to provide comfort and sustenance for the ever growing band of seafarers using the haven. Smithick, a name which could have been derived from St Mithick, was changed to the rather attractive and unusual name of Pennycomequick. This could have been a corruption of the Cornish names of Pen, Coomb and Ick, or more likely from the Celtic Pen y Cwm Gwic, meaning 'headland of the valley of the creek'; the creek referring to the area now known as the Moor.

There are some fascinating place names around Falmouth most of them having obvious connections with notable families of the area or the town's historical development. 'Pendennis' probably stems from 'Pen' and 'Dinas', meaning 'head of the fort', while 'Gyllyngdune' is thought to have been 'William's Height' and 'Gyllyngvase' is a derivation of 'William's Grave', for it is supposedly the burial place of Prince William, son of King Henry who was drowned on a passage from Normandy. The haven had been known as 'Falmouth' since the later Middle Ages and there was a proclamation during the first year of the reign of Charles II which stated that the town, 'in all times hereafter shall be called, named or known by the name of . . . Falmouth'. Just a year later, in 1661, the King granted the town its charter of incorporation and the Killigrews went ahead with constructing more quays and landing stages which greatly increased the town's business and prosperity. This was resented by the people of Penryn and Truro, for Falmouth's cornering of a greater share of the market effectively siphoned off their trade.

Already a thriving town, the establishment of a Post Office Packet Station in 1688 gave rise to what has been described as 'Falmouth's Golden Age'. At one time about forty vessels were operating as many as a hundred voyages a year. A special fleet of fast ships rigged as brigs with two masts carrying square sails, a long bowsprit, headsails and a large gaff mizzen sail were built locally, and in the early 18th century the ships sailed regularly to Spain, Portugal, the Mediterranean, the West Indies and the Americas. It was the leading Packet Station until the middle of the 19th century when the post office decided to send mail by steamship via Southampton. The packets, which also carried gold and silver coins and bullion were ready targets for attack by pirates and the whole enterprise was beset by privateers. Some of the most trusted and influential people around Falmouth were involved with smuggling, which had long been part of the way of life around the area. A Customs and Excise operation had been set up as early as 1652; a second building was erected on Custom House Quay in 1785 and the present, elegant Georgian building with its splendid coat of arms replaced it in 1814. Adjacent to the building still stands the 'King's Pipe' in which seized contraband goods were supposedly burnt. However, Falmouth folk were highly suspicious of the activities of certain Custom House officials, who, it was rumoured, grew stouter and richer.

'Falmouth For Orders' became a regular call for ocean going skippers and there was a growing need for fast, sturdy and efficient craft to ply the ship to shore service. Thus the world famous Falmouth Quay Punts evolved. Built locally, they were usually rigged as yawls with a gaff mainsail and Bermudan mizzen and were about thirty feet long. There was great competition to be the first to meet the incoming ships to secure business while the vessel was in port. These fine boats were built to last and some of them have sailed across the oceans of the world.

Falmouth is also famous for a slightly different breed of boat, used for oyster dredging in the winter months and for racing in the summer. Definitions are difficult, but originally known as the Truro River oyster boats, and something akin to the Falmouth Quay punts, these craft are now referred to as the Falmouth working boats. Rigged as gaff cutters with long bowsprits and billowing sails, these beautiful boats are a delightful reminder of the tradition of the great days of sail on the Falmouth waterfront.

The loss of the packet service brought about a decline in trade for Falmouth, but influential townsfolk who foresaw the potential of establishing a repair base with deep water wharves and dry docks formed the Falmouth Docks Company and acquired a suitable site for the construction of the docks in 1859. With an initial capital of £40,000 work went ahead on the first stages of the project.

By 1861 the Eastern Breakwater, Western Wharf and Number 1 Dry Dock were completed and in that year the first ship was berthed there. Number 2 Dry Dock was completed two years later, but financial difficulties followed.

A few years after the docks opened, two brothers, Joseph Goodenough Cox and Herbert Henry Cox started a ship chandlery business in the town, which expanded and moved to Western Wharf, becoming the Docks Foundry and Engineering Company in 1868. It later became an engineering and ship repairing firm known as Messrs. Cox & Co. (Engineers) Ltd. Thus began the ship repair organisation which became the main source of activity at the port.

With the coming of war in 1914 the Admiralty took over control of the docks, and when the dockyard became overloaded with war damaged ships Mr. John Silley, managing Director of Messrs. R. & H. Green & Silley Weir, Ltd. was called in as consultant. Large reinforcements of workmen were sent down from London to get repair work completed quickly. Up to this time two companies had worked together; one concerned with providing docking facilities for ships needing repair, the other carrying out repairs. Mr. Silley, aware of the potential of Falmouth Docks instigated negotiations with Messrs. Cox & Co. and with the Public Works Loan Commission and the representatives of the original shareholders with the result that the Falmouth Docks Co. and Messrs. Cox & Co. (Engineers) Ltd., passed into single ownership in 1918.

Following the amalgamation there was an intensive scheme of expansion, extension and reorganisation which rated Falmouth one of the most up-to-date and efficient ship repair yards in Europe. A few years after the transfer of ownership the name was changed to Silley, Cox & Co. Ltd. They were justifiably proud of their record of expansion, improvement and ability to keep abreast of the latest technology, and with the opening of the Queen Elizabeth Dock in 1958, Falmouth was equipped to receive some of the largest tankers in the world.

As a result of Falmouth's early commercial importance communications were good by land as well as by sea. By 1754 the turnpike road from Falmouth to Truro had been built and gates hung across the road to halt the traffic whilst the tolls were collected. The old turnpike toll cottages can still be seen along the route. In 1863 the railway between Truro and Falmouth was opened. Perhaps it was inevitable that a place so beautiful and well endowed as Falmouth, geared as it was to hospitality with its hotels, taverns and lodging houses, should have become so popular as a holiday resort in the middle of the 19th century. Murray's guide of 1865 attributes Falmouth's popularity primarily to the attractiveness of its position, 'as it mainly consists of one long narrow street, of a mean appearance, straggling along the side of the water'. However, it goes on to explain that the town had suffered greatly from a fire which had destroyed most of it in 1862. 'Of late years, however, Falmouth, like other towns, has been extended and improved, and there are now at either end of it, and on the heights above the shore, handsome and commodious dwellings, which command an uninterrupted view of the estuary.' Another guide printed in 1895 lists as hotels 'the *Falmouth*, close to the station and sea with *Pendennis* as an annexe; *Greenbank*, overlooking the harbour, nearly one and a half miles from the station; *Royal* and *Duke of Cornwall*, in Market Strand, about a mile from the station and *Lawson's Temperance*. . . ' which apparently required no further elaboration as to its merits.

Falmouth has long been famous for its mild, year-round climate where frost and snow are rare. The earlier guide draws attention to this, 'The climate of this town is remarkable for equability and mildness, in proof of which exotic plants flourish the year round in the open air. Mr. Fox of Grove Hill, obtained the Banksian medal for acclimatising upwards of 200 foreign plants. Orange and lemon trees are grown against the garden walls, and yield an abundant return of fruit.' Today, Falmouth's parks and gardens are a source of delight and regarded with great pride. The old guide books are fascinating to read and contain advice about safe bathing and the availability of bathing machines at Greenbank, yachting, pleasure trips by steamer, walks up Castle Drive and round other agreeable parts of this 'picturesque resting place'.

The haven, generally regarded as a safe and sheltered anchorage, provided a welcome sanctuary to a fleet of 300 vessels in 1815 when they took refuge from a fierce and terrible gale, riding it out in the Basin in the centre of Carrick Roads. All emerged unscathed. However, conditions can become treacherous, particularly when a southerly wind funnels up through the seaward headlands and sometimes when the wind is from landward. In 1814, in a strong southerly gale the transporter *Queen*, arriving home from the Peninsula with invalided soldiers, French prisoners, women and children aboard was driven from her anchors and dashed onto the rocks at Trefusis Point. In a desperate effort for survival the masts were sawn away and one fell on some of the terrified passengers; a few hours later the vessel disintegrated, and there was tremendous loss of life. Some of the victims were buried in Mylor, Budock and St Gluvias churchyards.

During the 19th century Falmouth coastguards, boatmen and volunteers displayed outstanding heroism in rescue work in the area, and the Lifeboat Institution's Gold Medal was awarded to them on several occasions, bringing honour to the town and creating a Cornish record. A number of incidents concerning shipping in distress between the 1820s and the middle of that century brought further recognition from the Institution. It is therefore rather surprising that, when the citizens of Gloucester who had collected money for a lifeboat to be built contacted Falmouth with a view to presenting it to the town, the mayor of the time responded by saying that in his opinion they did not require a lifeboat at Falmouth Harbour as it was so land-locked, but that the dangerous places along the coast to the south and east might well welcome the prospect of a lifeboat stationed nearby. Investigations carried out by Captain Ward, Inspector of lifeboats, failed to come up with a suitable alternative site, so the mayor called a meeting of the Town Council who put forward a resolution requesting him to accept the lifeboat *Gloucester*, and pledging that the town would look after her properly. Funds for a boathouse to be erected in the docks were raised by subscription and it was decided that the arrival of the new lifeboat should be an occasion to remember.

A committee formed by a number of influential gentlemen planned a colourful and triumphal procession through the streets to Penryn and along past Greenbank to the docks, and the presentation of the Albert Medal to a local seafaring hero. The Great Western Railway played its part by arranging to convey the lifeboat to Falmouth, free of charge.

In August 1867 Falmouth became a lifeboat station. The ten oared, self-righting lifeboat, *Gloucester*, arrived by rail before being mounted on a carriage and drawn through the streets by a team of 12 fine horses, beneath a billowing banner which proclaimed, 'SUCCESS TO THE GLOUCESTER LIFEBOAT'. The lifeboat crew sat on high wearing their cork lifebelts. It had been intended that the seamen and boys aboard the *Ganges* were to have joined in the colourful festivities and the march to Penryn, but for some reason the captain declined to let the boys take part in the procession, whereupon the people of Penryn also decided to drop out. Nevertheless, they were reported to have been impressed with the spectacle, and were enthusiastic about the whole thing. Having returned from Penryn to Greenbank, the dignitaries, guests and the bands reassembled themselves to parade onto the docks. The folk of Falmouth in their thousands lined the route and watched from the water, from doorways, balconies and windows. During the grand ceremony at the docks the medal for bravery was presented to Theophilus Jones, who was picked by the Queen to receive the award on behalf of all those who showed heroism rescuing disabled seamen from the ship *Marmion* on 17 March 1867, and there was a rousing rendition of 'See The Conquering Hero Comes'. During an exchange of speeches expressing suitable sentiments Mr. Lewis, Secretary of the Institution defied anyone to say that a lifeboat was not wanted in Falmouth. From that time the lifeboats including *Jane Whittingham, Bob Newbon, Jane Anne, Herbert Sturmy, The Brothers, B.A.S.P., Crawford and Constance Conybeare* and many relief lifeboats right up to the present day Arun Class *Elizabeth Ann*, have, together with generations of crewmen, performed distinguished service: and who could imagine Falmouth, this saltiest of old ports . . . without one?

On the westward side of the docks the area known as Bar Pool had been in industrial use from early times, and at the beginning of the 18th century two tide mills operated there. The water power was harnessed by closing the sluice gates at extreme high and low tides allowing the ensuing surge of water to set the mill wheels turning. Along the waterfront were blacksmiths, sailmakers and ropemakers. Malt was imported and beer was brewed for the many inns and hostelries; corn was ground into flour at local mills. There were fish cellars where pilchards were salted and pressed for export. The port also handled iron, timber, hemp, salt, tobacco, wines and spirits. At times Falmouth was reputed to have been rather a rough place and the genteel folk tended to favour Flushing.

Having established itself as a thriving place of many facets, banks, insurance companies and legal enterprises took root. In 1833 The Royal Cornwall Polytechnic Society, the first of its kind to be established in England, was founded, 'for the encouragement of the sciences, art and industry', and met in the town. By this time Falmouth was being recognised as quite a cultural centre with a theatre, coffee houses and reading rooms. In 1801 the population was said to be the largest of any town in the county and by 1861 it was an estimated 5,709.

On Sunday 5 January 1870 there was a serious fire in Market Street which got a firm hold before help was summoned. The Falmouth Fire Brigade arrived with a handpump but was unable to harness a supply of water; the Penryn Brigade used water from the harbour to quell the fire, while the men of H.M.S. *Ganges* attacked the blaze in spectacular style with a jet of water from their ship's pump, mounted on a pinnace. Falmouth folk rushed from their homes in their night attire and many business premises along the seaward side of the street were destroyed.

Since the end of the last century Falmouth and all nearby waterside places had their own special regattas which used to include swimming and water sports as well as sailing. There were sideshows and a variety of agreeable diversions to ensure that a good time was enjoyed by all. They used to enjoy model boat racing over at Swanpool and from Greenbank across to Flushing. Model making was taken very seriously and was a source of great pride; there are still a number of dedicated model-makers around who created exquisite, accurate replicas of the much loved sailing craft. Then, as now, winning trophies were prized and exhibited with pride.

Oyster dredging is thought to have been carried out in the estuary of the Fal and in the Truro River since Roman times and it was a way of life in these parts until the oyster disease struck in the early 1980s. The oysters spawned in summer and the working boats or oyster dredgers worked from October to March under licence. The dredges resembled a netted bag held open with a rigid framework which were dragged slowly along the bed of the river. A working boat with two men aboard was capable of towing four or five dredges along, but this had to be done slowly or the dredges would lift from the bottom and the whole operation would fail. The sails of the boat were set so that the boat would drift slowly, and the nets had to be hauled in carefully to avoid tangling. An oyster bailiff went around with a brass ring having an inside diameter of two and five-eighths inches; oysters smaller than this were to be returned to the water to mature. Generations of families along the Fal and its waterways have engaged in oyster dredging in a manner which has changed little since pre-Roman times.

Some of Falmouth's delightful 'Old Salts' who helped their fathers and grandfathers aboard some of the sailing vessels from a very tender age, and who themselves have seen service on schooners, quay punts, sailing barges and working boats can recall Custom House Quay as it was in the days of their youth. Impressive Topsail Schooners such as the *Snowflake, Earl Cairns, Alert* and *Mary Barrow* would come alongside the North Quay of Custom House Basin to discharge housecoal or roadstone in baskets which were then wheeled up the quay and offloaded onto the tip. Getting the vessels into the Basin was a highly skilled operation. Sometimes helped in by little local tugs they would wait on the outer side of the quay until the tide was suitable for them to drop back and their bowsprit cleared the southern end of the knuckle of the quay, enabling the men to grasp the bowsprit and pull the bow around to westward to enter the Basin and be winched into position by the granite bollard. The last vessel to be discharged there was the *Loch Ryan* at the end of November 1939. She was fated to become one of the first shipping casualties of the war for shortly afterwards she was strafed by a German bomber off the Lizard. Plymouth smacks, the *PHE, The Industry, The Yal* and ketches like the *Winifred*, the *Regina* and stone carrying barges including the *Sweet May, Silex, Dorothy, Eclipse, Kate, Mary, Emma* and the *Shamrock*, now restored and on display at Cotehele Quay, would have been a familiar sight as they passed upriver on their way from Porthoustock Quarries, down by the Manacles to the ports around the waterways of the Fal and its tributaries. In fact some of those sailing barges operated until just after the Second World War.

Through the centuries Falmouth has witnessed human conflict, but in the two World Wars of the 20th century it was on a rather more sophisticated scale. Pendennis Castle was once again fulfilling its original military function and batallions gathered in the area before boarding ships and being sent to the Front. The docks came under the jurisdiction of the Admiralty and the emphasis was on getting war-damaged ships repaired and back in the action as fast as possible. In the First World War Falmouth produced the famous 'Q' ships, and as a centre of Naval operations, particular attention was given to improving anti-submarine devices. In both wars the Germans displayed a close and detailed knowledge of the seabed around the area and even defied the dangers of the dreaded Manacles, scene of many shipwreck disasters. There are rumours of audacious Germans leaving their submarines to come ashore and enjoy the delights of the Falmouth nightlife, and rejoining their craft, undetected.

Falmouth, with its advantages of being near the Western Approaches, was chosen as a gathering place for the convoys as it reduced their chances of being hit going up the Channel. Food, oil and petroleum were all important. Naval boats patrolling in the area and decoy vessels intercepted enemy ships and took them back into the port.

In the period between the wars secret work was being carried out at Falmouth so that the port would be prepared, if another conflict should erupt. Part of the preparations involved a very large underground storage system with a network of flexible pipes, a forerunner of the Pluto pipeline to be evolved for the invasion of Europe some time later. With the outbreak of war on 3 September 1939, Falmouth Docks was ready to operate its planned wartime tactics.

Pamphlets were pushed through Falmouth letter boxes, giving civilians advice on how to cope with wartime situations, air raid precautions were set up and people were issued with gas masks, which had to be carried at all times. Glass in public buildings was covered on both sides with criss-cross guard tape and all windows had to be blacked out at night. Schoolchildren were instructed about the dangers of touching incendiary bombs, bullets, German parachutes and suspicious looking objects and told to seek help from someone in uniformed authority if in any doubt as to what to do. In times of danger they had to hasten to school, or homewards, or to the nearest place of refuge.

In the early part of the war people dug underground shelters in their gardens, or those who had no gardens took refuge in basements or under the stairs. Principal buildings in the area around the Moor were sandbagged and the place took on an alien appearance under an ocean of sandbags. An underground Command Post with slit openings, to allow surveillance of Falmouth Bay, was constructed on the site of the present *Membly Hall Hotel* at Gyllyngvase; Castle Point was sealed off for the duration, pill boxes were springing up everywhere and all beaches were sealed off with a network of scaffolding and barbed wire.

The threatening whine of approaching enemy aircraft became a familiar sound in Falmouth in 1940 and during the course of the war bombs were dropped on the dock-yard, the town and the waterways of the river where oil was being stored. In one raid Lister Street was almost wiped out and about eighteen people were killed. The area was roped off while the rescue services made a frantic effort to dig out survivors. Almost every day there were raids and at first there was little to defend the town from these air attacks, until the Royal Dutch Navy came along and 'let fly' at the marauders, with the result that the German 'planes took to flying higher. Armed trawlers were brought in and positioned around the haven. One daredevil German attacker was seen to fly his aircraft very low between Greenbank and Flushing with spray spinning off his propellers as he went in to attack the docks. Having hit a trawler he zoomed off over Pendennis and was gone.

After the evacuation of Dunkirk large numbers of ships converged on Falmouth and other ports along the south coast and disgorged thousands of exhausted servicemen of a variety of nationalities into the streets. There they lay on both sides of the streets, in shop doorways and corners, with kitbags for pillows and their weapons in the gutters. They had been days without sleep, but they were in England! Local people, short of rations themselves, took tea and refreshment to them and waited as the cups were gratefully received and passed around. Curious children were befriended by these men who gave them trophies such as coins, cap badges, buttons, bullets, German knives and all manner of things in return for the kindness shown. These treasures had to be returned to the police shortly afterwards.

After Dunkirk there was a lull and then the emphasis was on night time raids which were carried out by pairs of aircraft. They would fly in from Cherbourg or along the Brittany coast to attack shipping in the Channel. To intercept these attacks there were evening sorties from the network of Cornish airfields which were sited three or four miles apart.

Around 1941-2 a defensive barrage balloon system was set up with balloons at strategic points including Flushing, Trefusis Point, Pendennis, and the Beacon. This left the port open from the sea so the top structures were removed from the little old schooners and ketches and balloons were fixed from them to create floating barrage balloon bases. One of these, the ketch *Penryn*, was moored off the Prince of Wales Pier. Unfortunately British as well as German planes fell victim to this system. Around 1942 a Hudson crashed on the fitting shop in the dockyard and the crew was killed. There were a number of fatalities as the docks were regularly attacked day and night. Further upstream decoy lights were used to confuse the enemy as to the whereabouts of Truro and other strategic places. Malpas, where a large quantity of oil was stored, was narrowly missed on one occasion and the only casualty was a duck. After the war the *Falmouth Packet* newspaper printed a 1940 German map which gave exact details of the refinery.

Falmouth, traditional port of fishermen, set up a boom defence system to try and secure the loophole leaving them open to the sea, which was in effect a sort of metal fishing net strung between St Anthony Point and Pendennis Point and reaching to the bed of the estuary. There was a network of buoys linked to one ship which was anchored permanently and another system of buoys linked to a second ship which would allow legitimate traffic through by steaming across and opening a movable section forming a 'gate'. The Germans retaliated to this development by dropping mines inside the harbour from their aircraft. One little coaster which was seen to be struck by a German mine was destroyed, amidst a jet of water thrust high into the air. Other vessels rushed to her aid in vain. It was a familiar sight to see convoys forming in Falmouth Bay, waiting with their escorts and taking about a week to prepare, the water becoming black with silhouettes before they suddenly dispersed leaving the bay strangely empty.

Older Falmouth folk can well remember the arrival of the Americans around 1943 and it seemed to them that they took over everything. The place seemed to be packed out with Americans and their equipment. A 'town' of prefabricated huts and structures appeared to mushroom up on the Beacon almost overnight, across acres and acres of fields where houses now stand. The local people accustomed to rationing and doing without luxuries were somewhat bemused with the arrival of these noisy extroverts who seemed to have plenty of everything. There was a good rapport between them and the locals . . . a bit too good at times for a number of Falmouth girls became pregnant. The Americans had gum, cigarettes, candies, cigars, chocolate, tinned meats, tropical fruits, Horlicks tablets and all manner of good things which the youngsters had never seen before. What they did not want they would throw or give away. Local people carried out services for them such as sewing and laundering; transactions would be arranged at the camp gates and if money was not exchanged they would pay 'in kind'. It has been reported that 'USN' sheets and blankets were seen flapping from many a Falmouth line long after the end of the war.

In 1944 everybody knew that things were building up to a climax, but exactly what or when was not known. A school of firefighting had been set up at Swanpool, replacing the old mine workings; a mock-up of an engine room had been constructed with two storeys, ladders and a vast quantity of oil beneath and this was where firefighting instruction was carried out. One night the place was set on fire after receiving a direct hit as 14 enemy aircraft flew across. It was a desperate situation, saved by an American negro in an act of heroism which went unrecognised.

Sparks were flying in other directions too, for pent up Canadians arriving off the convoys having experienced hard times, death and disaster were frustrated to come ashore and find the Americans, who they felt had not yet proved themselves, propping up Falmouth bars and having their way with the local girls. After a few drinks there were sometimes punch-ups in the bars, followed by wild rampages through the streets leaving trails of destruction.

As D-day drew near bulks of gear, landing craft and vehicles seemed to fill the place. The tension was mounting. Ships filled the harbour; there was a strange blend of heightened activity and waiting. . . . Suddenly they went away . . . but were back next morning. This happened two or three times. Then, suddenly they went away . . .

Falmouth had to adjust to life without the Americans. On V.E. night in 1945, as people all over the country celebrated, the ships of many nationalities in Falmouth let fly with a colourful and memorable display of flares and rockets, fired in joy. Many families waited for their loved ones to return from their particular war experiences, and some were not so lucky.

But at various times throughout history there must have been those who would re-echo W. E. Henley's uncomplicated sentiment:

'O Falmouth is a fine town with ships in the Bay
And I wish in my heart it's there I was today.'

The Plates

1. This rather romanticised lithograph depicts the view from St Mawes Castle to its twin fort of Pendennis crowning the headland. At the time of Henry VIII there were plans to build two further fortresses, one at Gyllyngvase and the other at Trefusis, to protect ships in the haven and the access to the ports of Penryn and Truro.

The Haven from Three Points of View

2.   From Pendennis looking north-westwards to Falmouth town. Murray's 1865 *Guide* states: 'This town, seated on shore of one of the finest harbours in the kingdom, derives its principal interest in the beauty of its position, as it mainly consists of one long narrow street, of a mean appearance, straggling along the side of the water.'

3.   A south-easterly angle, looking down the haven to the sea beyond emphasises the dominance of Pendennis. The squat form of St Mawes Castle can be seen on the headland to the left of the chimneys. The further headland of St Anthony is the natural demarcation of the entrance to the estuary. The foreground depicts an idyllic, rural scene.

Early Days

The John Killigrew
orial in Budock
ch. John Killigrew, of
nack, Lord of the
or was responsible for
arly development of
outh. He was the
Captain of Pendennis
e.

HEERE LYETH IOHN KILLIGREW: ESQVIER, OF
ARWENACK, AND LORD OF Y MANOR OF KILLIGREW
IN CORNEWALL, AND ELIZABETH TREWINNARD HIS
WIFE, HE WAS THE FIRST CAPTAINE OF PENDENNIS
CASTLE, MADE BY KING HENRY THE EIGHT, & SO CONTI
NVED VNTILL THE NYNTH OF QVEENE ELIZABETH
AT WHICH TIME GOD TOOKE HIM TO HIS MERCYE,
BEING THE YEARE OF OVR LORD 1567
S IOHN KILLIGREW KNIGHT HIS SOÑE. SVCCEEDED HIM
IN Y SAME PLACE BY THE GIFT OF QVEENE ELIZABETH

5.   This granite obelisk was erected by Martin Killigrew in memory of Sir John Killigrew. It was placed in the Grove in 1737, removed to the area now known as Lansdowne Road in 1836 and came to this waterside site near Arwenack House in 1871.

6.   An early drawing of Arwenack Manor, seat of the Killigrew family, who were not averse to a bit of smuggling and piracy in pursuit of power and wealth. In the Civil War the house was partly destroyed, and it was taken over by Parliamentarians to base their assault on Pendennis.

7. (*overleaf above*) Pendennis Castle has weathered the centuries and been put to its test. Built by Henry VIII as part of a south coast defensive system, it held out for a six-month siege under the command of 87-year-old John Arundell in 16 and has re-assumed its military function in times of subsequer national crisis.

8. (*overleaf below*) The cannon and the pale and delicate primrose in poignant juxtaposition at Pendennis. These canno were used aboard warships. Cannon balls were embedded in brass triangular structures known as 'monkeys'. In freezing conditions the contracting metal would cause the cannon ball to eject from their brass monkeys; hence the expression 'to freeze the balls off a brass monkey'.

9. (*left*) Devon-born Sir Walter Raleigh was among the first t recognise the potential of the haven, and Sir John Killigrew, seeing the economic advantages of this, pressed ahead with th construction of new quays. Ale houses began to spring up, serving the needs of the increasing number of seafarers using port.

10 (*below*) Facsimile of the Warrant to execute King Charles 1648. The town, which was loyal to the King, received its Charter of Incorporation in 1661, in the second year of the re of Charles II. Falmouth's rise in importance brought about th decline of formerly prosperous Penryn and Truro as ports.

FAC-SIMILE OF WARRANT TO EXECUTE KING CHARLES I.

11.   During the Civil War Charles I was a hunted man, but Pendennis was a Royalist stronghold and provided sanctuary for Queen Henrietta Maria and others. Later the town received its charter and the parish church was dedicated to King Charles the Martyr. This photograph shows its beautiful east window.

12. The barquentine *Mozart* at 'Falmouth for Orders'.

13. The sturdy, flamboyant and indefatigable packet boat captain, John Bull, who successfully weathered many a se faring skirmish, was probably the inspiration for the legendary and patriotic notion of 'John Bull'. Having commande two packet ships named the *Duke of Marlborough*, he came ashore and named his fine house Marlborough House. Th scene is from an engraving.

14. The former tide mill at Bar Pool which was activated by the rise and fall of the tide dated from 1690. Here the corn was ground, loaded on barges and taken away by water. This is how it looked around the middle of the last century. It was demolished in 1914.

Views

A view across Gyllyngvase to Swanpool with its stack, and the entrance to Helford River beyond. Notice the
[g]leman intent with his telescope. Could he be looking for Morgawr, the monster of Falmouth Bay? Morgawr,
[who] has been sighted in the area over the last few hundred years, favours calm conditions and hot summers for an
[app]earance.

16.   Falmouth from Flushing around 1900. On a calm day, set against the handsome background of the Falmouth waterfront, sailing vessels and tugs go about their daily business. The old observatory can be seen on the skyline and the Catholic church steeple is identifiable, but it is prior to the electric light works and Prince of Wales Pier.

17.   Across the railway line to the left of the picture was the site of the former tide mill, and County Wharf is now where the two-masted schooner lies. The *Chain Locker Inn* and *Boatman's House* are discernible on Custom House Quay. The Killigrew Monument, the old weather observatory and Victoria Cottages can also be seen.

Greenbank, the probable site of Pennycomequick, was named, so the whimsical story goes, after the lady inn-keeper who, having brewed beer for a special celebration for her 'regulars', sold it all to some Dutch sailors, unable [to] resist the tempation of such a quick turnover. 'The penny come so quick,' she explained. Across the water is [Fla]shing.

All set fair at the mouth of the haven with fine, summertime weather, cumulus clouds and deep water sailing [ship]s at anchor. The flag above St Anthony Lighthouse indicates a north-westerly wind, but the floodtide swings [the] stern of the ships to the north'ard. Notice the old bell on the lighthouse which was later removed.

20. This 1901 view along Gyllyngvase Beach to Swanpool with *Falmouth Hotel* on the right appears somewhat sparse and deserted by modern day standards. During the Second World War an underground lookout was constructed near the centre of this picture, and a bomb hit a building killing a number of American servicemen and their girlfriends.

21. Local folk and holidaymakers have always taken pleasure in the unique and delightful situation of the haven where each direction presents a pleasing aspect. In 1901, when this picture was taken, it was only the 'well heeled' who could enjoy holidays, as these two gentlemen are obviously doing.

Developing around the shores of the haven
up the side of the hill, Falmouth, with its
⊃ terrain, is characterised by terraces linked
teps and narrow slipways. Jacob's Ladder with
12 steps is situated beside the Wesleyan chapel.
picture dates from around 1903. It is
·esting to observe the children's fashions.

Tree-lined Arwenack Avenue, formerly the
ᴇ to the Manor House, as it looked in 1903.
was the old rope walk where rope was
·essed and spun. There was a long shed and
·red way allowing space to make two sixty-
om lengths of rope in one continuous line.
industry finished around 1895.

24. Flushing, with its charming Dutch-influenced architecture, was favoured by the genteel set when Falmouth town was a bit on the rough side! However, Falmouth changed its image with the founding of the Polytechnic Society, with coffee houses, reading rooms and stylish hotels including the Greenbank, seen in the picture, adjacent to the quayside on the right.

25. It's low tide at Gyllyngvase Beach in June 1912, with bathing huts on the sands and just a handful of folk enjoying summertime delights. Meanwhile, up on Castle Drive it's a case of a photographer (Herbert Hughes) photographing a photographer apparently right in the firing line as he contemplates his own 'shot' across to Swanpool and Pennance Point.

'The calm before the storm', as this photograph from Marine Drive looking towards Pendennis in 1912 demonstrates. The commanding castle of Pendennis stands in noble profile on the headland as it has done for centuries, resuming its defensive, military role in times of strife.

A pause for tranquil reflections of the past in Custom House Basin. This delightful study was captured by very talented photographer, Herbert Hughes on 12 July 1912.

28. A 1938 photograph of the delightful single storey cottage, aptly named 'The Retreat', at Swanpool. It was a building of individuality and charm with interesting chimneys and fascinating undulating roof contours.

29. The lead mine at Swanpool opened in 1852 and the sulphide and arsenical content had to be removed before smelting. A long tunnel led to Pennance Point where there was a tall chimney stack giving rise to noxious effluvium. A second tunnel was constructed for better ventilation, but there were problems, and the mine, running at a loss, was closed.

30. The derelict mine at Swanpool with its waste tip was beloved by small boys on bikes who whizzed around and performed amazing tricks all over it. It was removed by US forces in the last war to make way for a school of fire-fighting. It is now the basis of Swanpool car park.

. Swanpool has traditionally been a recreational area for local folk of every class. In this tasteful and graceful ne, some of the members of the 'upper crust' share a few crumbs with the resident swan population.

32. To the left of this 1880 drawing of Lower Killigrew Street was *Ralph's Temperance Hotel*, which was conveniently situated opposite Devenish's Brewery.

33. Falmouth market stalls at the Moor, 1890, on the site of the present market.

Street Scenes

The approach to Falmouth station, opened in 1863, sets the scene for a delightfully winsome and coy photographic child study. We shall never know what he said to her or how she replied! The hotels sent horse-buses to meet guests off the trains.

35. Sir Peter Killigrew's Custom House, with the fine coat of arms above the portals, as it looked at the turn of the century. In those early days of photography it was quite an event to see a photographer at work, and willing subjects would adopt a lengthy pose for the duration of the exposure. Arwenack Street has changed very little.

36. Looking down Quay Hill from outside Oddfellows, with the *Dolphin Hotel* on the right (now closed). To the left was Blackers the barber's shop, long since closed.

. John Burton, the flamboyant proprietor of The Old Curiosity Shop, started in a small way with china and
ts and pans, but the collecting bug took hold of him and he travelled far and wide to secure every kind of
likely object, the most bizarre being the boat involved in the notorious and grisly cabin boy/cannibalism
ident.

. (*overleaf*) The main route into Falmouth town was formerly past Greenbank and down High Street, where
ge families lived in tenement blocks. The buildings to the left commanded fine views across the harbour.

39. An imaginative photographer achieved a pleasing under-the-arch, well-framed picture of the decorative timber-built chalet-style lodge house at the Dell, known to one and all as 'Swiss Cottage'. This gate house to the Grove Hill Estate is now taken up by a car park.

40. Situated on the old route into Falmouth, *Greenbank Hotel* was one of the first hotels to be built. An established part of Falmouth history, it displays fascinating old pictures and relics. From here Kenneth Grahame wrote imaginative letters to his young son, from which evolved *The Wind In The Willows*. The letters were addressed to 'My Darling Mouse...'.

Buildings

41. A domestic scene outside the front of 48 High Street, an area which was later cleared. Mariners returned from the sea, happy to be home with their wives and families, and would sit at their windows with telescopes trained on waterfront activities, looking forward to the dreaded day of the family parting. Such is the bitter-sweet call of the sea.

42. *Falmouth Hotel* was built once the railway link put the town on the map as a resort. In those days only the more privileged people in society had the means to travel and take holidays. *Falmouth Hotel* still offers the opportunity of an English seaside holiday with immaculate style.

43. A 1936 rear view of buildings at Smithick Hill in an area then due for clearance. Falmouth had long had the tradition of the very rich and the very poor with few bridging the gulf between.

44. Boatman Walter Morrison, who had 10 children, lived in this Gyllyng Street house. The daughters became tailoresses; the boys became boatmen and one joined the Navy. Buildings in the street were pulled down in the 1970s to the regret of former residents who said the walls were three feet thick and there was no trace of dampness.

45. An imaginative angle on the attractive rooftops and chimneys of Cliff Place in 1937. These buildings of great character and charm were all demolished. Planners these days are more aware of the individuality and beauty of local architecture, and aim to renovate rather than desecrate.

46.   The 10-oared sail/row lifeboat *Jane Whittingham*, which was on station from 1887 to 1894, with her crew. Seco[ ]
from left (in trilby hat) is Lifeboat Secretary Mr. Moseley. Standing in the boat (far left, with moustache) is George
Jones. In the background steam and sail are visible, with Lowestoft and other fishing smacks which called at the fish-
market 'after the 'erring'.

47.   Crew members of the 12-oared, self-righting *Bob Newbon*, which functioned from 1894 to 1922, included Mr.
Morrison, 'Slasher' Jones, Wally Brown and Willy Tompkin. The crew are in working clothes, wearing cork life-jackets[ ]
and the rest are helpers and launchers. This lifeboat was called to the *Mohegan* disaster in 1898, S.S. *Paris* in 1899 an[ ]
to the barque *Hera* in 1914.

Falmouth Lifeboat

Crowds gathered around the lifeboat and her crew when they returned to port with five survivors after ending the wreck of *Hera* of Hamburg, returning from a 91-day voyage. On 31 January 1914, *Hera* went course and struck the Whelps reef in Gerrans Bay, sinking within 10 minutes. The lifeboat crew included Jones brothers and Reggie Tonk.

49.   After the launching of the new Watson lifeboat *Crawford & Constance Conybeare* in 1940, the crew and her donor, Mrs Conybeare of London, pose for the photographer. *From left to right:* 1 William 'Bill' Brown; 2 Leonard Morrison; 3 Herbert 'Chiefie' Williams (Engineer); 4 Jack 'Janner' Snell (Coxswain); 5 Mrs Conybeare (Donor); 6 Wally Jarvis (Journalist & Secretary to the Lifeboat); 7 Sidney 'Squibs' Timmins; 8 Tom Sault

50.   Outside his High Street home, former Coxswain Arthur 'Toby' West, who follows in the wake of such illustrious men as Janner Snell, Charlie Brown and Bertram West reflects on a colourful seafaring past, in the tradition of his forebears.

Falmouth Docks

51.   The potential for a dockyard had been recognised in the 1820s by local businessmen of vision. This delightful artist's impression of the future dockyard reflecting pride in artistry and engineering, now hangs in the
Chairman's office. 'FALMOUTH HARBOUR SHEWING WORKS of DOCK COMPANY to be Completed in
1866. JAMES ABERNETHY ESQ. CHIEF ENGINEER J.R. KELLOCK RESIDENT ENGINEER.'

52.   Masts and funnels in evidence at the docks in 1887. A large barque and two other vessels share the basin. The dockyard has always been justifiably proud of keeping abreast with developing technology.

53.   A charcoal-sketched 'seagull's eye' view of the docks (Cox & Co., Engineers, Ltd.) in 1919. It seems to some that the local seagull population gets larger and more aggressive. Rumour has it that workers wear hard hats in defence against marauding seagulls.

1919
Falmouth
Docks.
Cox & Co.
Engineers
Limited.

. The development of the docks effectively filled a void left by the loss of the Packet Service to Southampton.
 the beginning of the First World War Mr. John Silley was summoned to Falmouth to organise repair work of
ar-damaged ships. He stayed on; the company passed into single ownership in 1918, and later became Silley,
ox & Co. Ltd.

5. (overleaf above) The dream has become a reality...with modifications. This early aerial photograph taken from the
posite direction demonstrates the success of the venture when 'steam' was ousting 'sail'. In the foreground *Falmouth*
otel stands in splendid isolation in an area now mostly covered by buildings. The railway line and old station are near
e centre of the photograph.

5. (overleaf below) Emergency at Falmouth Docks on 21 January 1908, when S.S. *Strathlyon* caught on fire.

57. A stern view of a straight-funnelled London-based steamship in dry dock on 24 February 1922. The distinctive shape of the *Falmouth Hotel* can be seen in the background.

58. This expressive and compelling study of human effort, in the days before machines took over, conveys more than words ever could. Thus we share with them the experience of excavation work at the docks around the 1940s, which in the modern vernacular might be described as 'hard graft'.

59.   Built in 1890 as a passenger liner, S.S. *Highland Fling* was converted for cargo carrying. Following repairs at Falmouth she ran onto rocks near Cadgwith in fog on 7 January 1907. With her bow embedded in rocks, she was cut in two and her stern section was brought to Falmouth. She was beyond repair.

60.   Around Christmas 1927, in terrifying blizzard conditions, the ketch barge *Lady Daphne*'s master was lost overboard and her helpless crew was rescued by the Lizard lifeboat. Abandoned, she 'centred on' until she ran herself neatly ashore on sand at Tresco. Astonished lifeboatmen at St Mary's discovered her only occupant to be a canary singing in a cage. She was brought to Falmouth for repairs.

To Falmouth for Repairs

Having had her nose put out of joint, *Samos* limped into port where a close assessment was made as to the
extent of the damage to her crumpled bow.

Shipping Round the Harbour

2. (*opposite*) The Royal Navy training ship H.M.S. *Ganges*, built in Bombay in the early 19th century, was ased at the Royal Naval Dockyard upstream at Mylor from 1886 to 1899.

3. (*above*) Wistful expressions on the faces of the boy sailors of the *Ganges* in 1890. Many of them were rphans and they led a harsh life aboard. At the time of the arrival of the lifeboat the lads from *Ganges* were to ave taken part in the procession, but for some reason their captain disallowed this at the last moment.

64. The frigate *Foudroyant*, formerly *Trincomalee*, was built in Bombay in 1817. At the beginning of this century she was brought to Falmouth and adapted as a training ship for boys. She was moved to Portsmouth in 1929.

65. The first *Victoria*, built by Cox & Company in 1900, was sold within the same year. The second *Victoria*, built in 1901, was sold to Portugal in 1906. *Roseland*, lying aft, also built by Cox & Company, operated from 1886 to 1945.

. The perky, tall-funnelled craft in the foreground is the Flushing ferry *Express*. Lying aft is the first *Queen of Fal*. The background with masts and funnels captures the early transition from sail to steam around 1908.

. The two-funnelled, Falmouth-built tug *Penguin* was a familiar sight around the harbour until about 1914.

68. The first *Queen of the Fal*, built by Cox & Company, operated from 1893 to 1911. She was replaced by the second *Queen of the Fal* (pictured here) in 1912 which functioned until 1942. In the Second World War she was used as a patrol vessel/tender to the troop ships.

69. The trading ketch *Eclipse*, built by Rapson who had a yard below St Gluvias church at Mano Meads, Penryn, used to carry loa of up to 60 tons of stone, coal or anything which needed transport In 1890 her first cargo of barley went from Penryn to Gweek.

. Custom House Basin has seen many changes in the last 50 years. In the 1930s and earlier there was a procession
vessels entering the basin to discharge housecoal or roadstone onto the quay, where it was left in heaps, as seen
re. The sailing barge *Regina* operated around the coast and to ports up-river.

. Topsail schooners, including *Snowflake, Earl Cairns, Alert* and *Mary Barrow*, seen here around 1920 discharged
rgo on Custom House Quay. The crew loved the life and took pride in their ships. Notice the stylish figurehead and
e immaculate appearance, despite the messy cargo. *Mary Barrow*, built in Falmouth by Leans, was wrecked on the
e of Man around 1935.

72. Stern view of two fine old ladies, *Foudroyant* and, forward of her, the Tea Clipper *Cutty Sark*, sailing under another name and dressed overall. She was purchased by Captain Dowman and restored and remained in the port until 1938. She was later to become a maritime exhibit at Greenwich.

H.M.S. *Implacable* was a familiar sight around Falmouth in the early 1920s. Usually moored in St Just Pool, she s temporarily moved to King Harry Reach in 1922/23.

The steam tug *Northgate Scott* in 1926/28 with *Cutty Sark* in the background and Coastlines Shipping Company -loading onto lighters, which are the smaller vessels to each side of her. *Northgate Scott*, later renamed *St Denys*, s to see service in Custom House Basin as Falmouth's Floating Museum.

75. *Princess Maud (left)* of the St Mawes Company was a mail ship for the Roseland area and carried the Royal Mail insignia to the fore of her funnel. *New Resolute*, owned by the River Fal Steamship Company, Falmouth, was built at Malpas in 1882 and operated around the harbour until 1927.

Fishing

76. Fish Strand Quay was aptly named for it was the landing place for fish and the site of the busy local fish market. The men and boys were obviously eager to be photographed, but the lady on the right seems a trifle coy. An evocative view of old Falmouth. Today this area adjoins the Church Street car park.

77. 'And sweet it is across the tide
    To hear the fisher's song...' (From the poem *On Falmouth*, by John Harris)

78. The fishing fleet has returned and the catch is being landed in baskets at the water's edge before being loaded onto horse-drawn carts and taken to the fish market. Fishing smacks came from Lowestoft, Brixham and all over the south-west.

79. Here we see Jimmy Morrison and Eddie Roberts sailing back over the drift to start dredging again, in Jimmy's boat *Mayflower*...a traditional wintertime activity in Carrick Roads where methods can have changed little since Roman times. The vessels need a shallow draught to allow them to drift back over the oyster beds.

80. Shadows of inactive masts and rigging cast patterns across each other in the early morning sunshine, whilst funnels across the water puff up jets of white steam in eager readiness for action. The lady on the quay grasping the baby is wearing substantial button boots.

81. *Boy Willie* alongside Fish Strand Quay in the 1920s with a very young
George Vinnicombe in the stern of his father's boat. This 150-year-old, 31-
footer, built at Porthleven, was converted from a pilchard smack to motor-
ised vessel and then to oyster dredger. The Vinnicombes moved from Devon
to Mylor, attracted by the oyster dredging several generations ago.

Transport and Services

. In the days when errand boys whistled cheerfully on their daily round, one of Maypole's well turned-out
ls, who had presumably finished his dockyard deliveries, pauses to admire the lines of a very graceful lady.
dly, *Pamir*, a steel grain ship went down in the Atlantic with the loss of all hands.

83.　Mail coaches kept to a strict schedule with fast dispatch riders on horseback catching them up with urgent communications. This picture, taken from an old print, depicts the last mail coach leaving Market Strand in 1863, when the railway opened. It was the end of an era.

84.　The *Royal Artillery Militia* at Pendennis Castle in 1890 looking proud and resplendent, proving then, as now, just what a stylish uniform can do for a man!

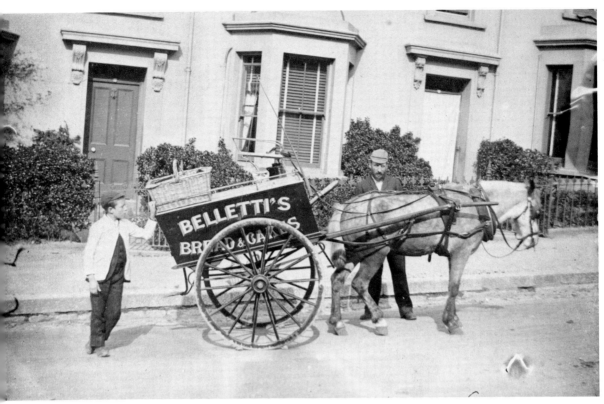

85. The camera catches an early work-a-day scene in a Falmouth street as two of Belletti's staff pause in the delivery of their daily bread. Notice the pleasingly designed cart and its beautifully fashioned wheels.

All eyes were on the cameraman as the first passenger car prepared to leave Falmouth on Easter Monday, 1904. e passengers enjoyed weather protection, but there were no windscreens in those days as they were regarded as a ety hazard, impairing the vision of the driver in dark and rainy conditions. Luggage was stowed up aloft.

87.   Outside Prince of Wales Pier around 1910 neatly aligned horse cabs and cabbies await business. In the days of the *Lake* family, the *Falmouth Packet* newspaper operated from the building on the left and on the right is the *King's Hotel*. Shadowy silhouettes of topsail schooners can be seen out on the harbour.

88.   This attractive Lacre 18 h.p. blue van was acquired by Rickeards of Penryn as their laundry service vehicle. Noti the protective clothing worn by the two roundsmen. The canvas canopy provided some weather protection for them.

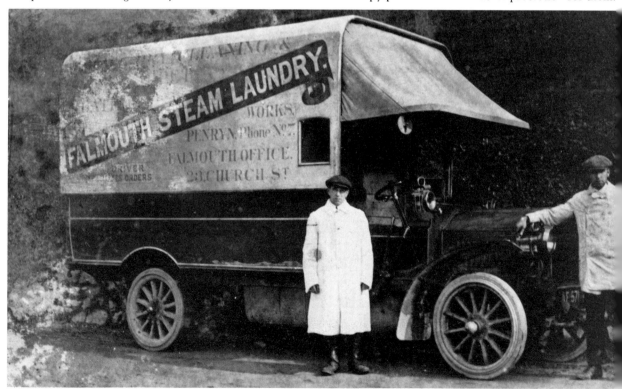

A policeman's lot...policemen who served in the Falmouth area between 1900 and 1913, looking well turned but a bit apprehensive of the camera, an unfamiliar object at that time.

Falmouth Fire Brigade with their new fire engine, which had a steam pump acquired in 1910, being nonstrated on the Moor. There was some delay in tackling the blaze because of the need to get up sufficient am for it to operate.

91. There is a blend of anticipation and formality as the first Penryn to Falmouth Lacre 40 h.p. charabanc, owned by the Penryn & Falmouth Company, prepares for take off in 1912. It was the first privately owned Cornish bus.

92. The Mayor and members of St John Ambulance Brigade welcome the arrival of Falmouth's first ambulance outside Passmore Edwards' Free Library. The horses look pert and proud, and the vehicle is immaculate with its fine craftsmanship. Simon Gay, a horse-drawn cabbie by profession, used his horses for the fire brigade and ambulance services.

93. Well situated near the dockyard entrance, Belletti's garage provided employment and enjoyment for many, by land and by water. These proudly displayed new cars, now vintage models, would delight the heart of any modern day motor enthusiast. A notice board advertises 'Chara Tours' around the area.

4. There was great jubilation when the railway was opened on 21 August 1863, with processions, parades, banners and flowers. Thousands of local folk welcomed the Company's Directors, who arrived by special train from Truro, with a reception at the station followed by an evening banquet. In 1892 the line between Exeter and Falmouth was converted from broad to narrow gauge.

95. Secret experimental underwater work was carried out with submarines and anti-submarine devices in the First World War. Submarine Pier, constructed by the War Office in conjunction with the adjacent Royal Engineers' Barrack was purchased by the docks in 1929. It was requisitioned by the War Office in 1941 and retained by them until 1957.

96. H.M.S. *Falmouth*, a 2nd Class cruiser, sailing down the haven at the beginning of the First World War.

Recollections of War

. The camera has caught a comprehensive view and captured the ominous atmosphere of Falmouth in the First
orld War as warships gather in the historic bay in readiness for conflict; a situation that the town has known through-
t its history in its 'first in...last out' geographical situation.

98. Following the First World War various wartime relics were displayed around the town for several years. This old tank, which came in under its own power, provided an unusual adventure playground for the young (and not so young!) It was later cut up for scrap by Harris, the scrap-merchants.

99. The old torpedo boat *Ardent* was broken up for scrap on the beach at Falmouth. At various times an assortment of wartime vessels were dumped on the beaches arousing local interest and curiosity before being broken up and taken away for scrap.

100. *St Gerrans*, built in 1927 and one of the first with diesel engine, was difficult to start. Once started, her cylinder head needed warming by blowlamp. That achieved, there was difficulty in engaging reverse. Commandeered for wartime service, she was a puzzle to Plymouth personnel, who in desperation returned her to Falmouth to those who understood her temperament.

A stick of bombs caused devastation at the dockyard in July 1940. *British Chancellor* took the brunt in her ... ne room; the tanker *Tuscaloosa* sank where she was and the fully-loaded Greek cargo ship *Marie Chandris* was ... ed to St Mawes and scuppered to put out the fire. Charles Pears' fine painting hangs in the Boardroom today.

2. A fascinating and ...phic dockyard composite ...otograph shows what was ...t of *British Chancellor* ...er the bombs had struck ...r engine room. (The popu-...Falmouth story is that the ...mbs went straight down ...r funnel into the engine ...om.) Despite all this dam-...e she was repaired at the ...ckyard.

S.T. "BRITISH CHANCELLOR"
BOMB DAMAGE
FALMOUTH JULY 1940.

103. *(left)* The *Wings for Victory* parade outside the Municipal Buildings in the Moor in 1940. This was an opportunity for civilians to 'do their bit' for the war effort in raising money.

104. *(below)* Tony Warren's painting depicts a composite scene of Second World War craft around Falmouth. Ketches became barrage balloon anchors. Also shown: Air Sea Rescue launch; LSTs carrying assault landing craft; Right; D U W K (DUCK), amphibious truck comes in. The floating crane was removed, having become a 'fix' for the FW 190's who strafed and bombed the docks. Notice convoy escort destroyers.

105. *(opposite above)* A large American camp appeared on the Beacon and officers took over houses, hotels (and some of the girls) concrete landing stages were constructed here and upstream. At Falmouth it was tension, heightened activity, uncertainty and waiting as D Day approached. Local folk who had built up a good rapport with the 'Yanks' found things strangely quiet after their departure.

106. *(opposite below)* 'Yes, we have no bananas...' was the usual situation in wartime Britain and many British children had never set eyes on bananas or tropical fruits in their lives; but bananas and smiles are bountiful aboard the American army landing craft at Falmouth, prior to D Day.

ST. MARY'S CATHOLIC CHURCH.
FALMOUTH.

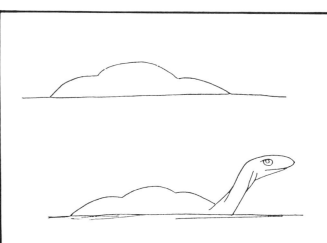

107. *(left)* The first Roman Catholic church was at Greenbank
The church of St Mary Immaculate in Killigrew Street, opened
1869 and consecrated in September 1948, narrowly escaped a
bomb in 1941 which demolished the buildings opposite. This
photograph was taken in the 1920s.

108. *(above)* There have long been stories of a monster in
Falmouth Bay and the press has reported sightings since 1876.
George Vinnicombe, fishing in the bay, was astonished when w
he thought was a grey, upturned boat suddenly raised a serpent
like head. It was 17 feet long and had three humps. Gasped
George, 'Must be Old Nick!'.

109. *(below)* The Bethel Sailors' Rest, with the pulpit fashion
like the bow of a ship, was nautical and practical in that it con-
cealed the bellows of the pipe organ. Above is the inscription:
'The abundance of the sea shall be converted unto Thee'.

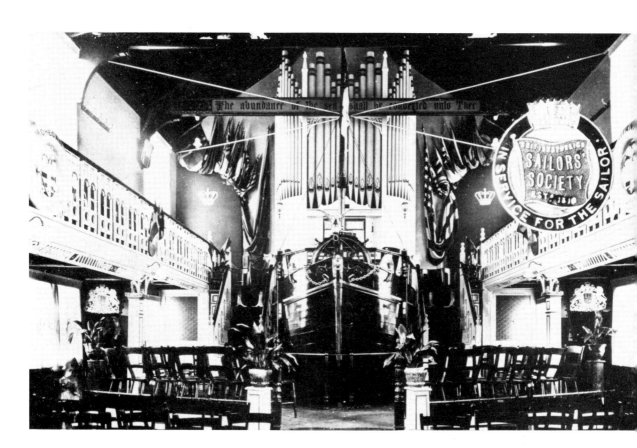

Institutions, Events and Happenings

. The first observatory, a distinctive tower-like landmark, was erected in 1868, but it was replaced in 1885
h this observatory on Western Terrace. The revolving anamometer recorded windforce and indicated direction.
: mild and equable climate allowed exotic plants to grow outdoors all the year round. Falmouth has long been
ud of its tradition of colourful parks and gardens.

111.   The chapel on the Gyllyngdune Estate, bought by General W.J. Coope, was said to have been used for private prayer and meditation. Father of the rector of Falmouth, he was killed in a carriage accident following his son's induction service. Some historians insist that the place was built as a summerhouse/bathing shelter, and was never used as a chapel.

112.   Osborne Studios in Arwenack Street, otherwise known as 'Ossie's Shop', founded by Maurice Osborne's grandfather 'Boss' (who was reputed never to be without a cigar), built up a fascinating collection of photographs over 100 years, some of which can be seen in this book. Outside the premises in 1920 are Doris and Lucy Campbell, Leslie Osborne and Ruby Butland.

113. The fire in High Street which destroyed 30 houses on 12 April 1862. Murray's 1865 *Guide* states: 'Falmouth (Pop. in 1861, 5,709) suffered much from a fire in 1862 which destroyed a considerable portion of the town'.

114. On 5 January 1870 a fire started in Market Street and spread rapidly in all directions. The Falmouth Fire Brigade experienced difficulty in harnessing a water supply; the Penryn brigade was more successful, but it was the men from H.M.S. *Ganges* who were effective in producing a spectacular jet from the seaward side from their deck-pump mounted on a pinnace.

115. Representatives of Falmouth's young manhood awaiting starter's orders outside the *Falmouth Hotel* for the 'Round the Houses' race. A cluster of interested spectators divide their attentions between the athletes and the cameraman. Notice the distinctive style of footwear, headgear and shorts.

116. The four-masted barque *The Bay of Panama* was one of many ships which met with disaster in the Great Blizzard of March 1891. The Captain, his wife and others were swept overboard to their deaths by a huge wave. Some were rescued from the freezing rigging by breeches buoy.

117. H.M.S. *St Vincent,* one of the last wooden Dreadnoughts was a 1st rate ship built at Devonport in 1815 and named after the Admiral of the Fleet. Battle Honours: Baltic 24th March 1854; Became RN Reserve Ship 1859; & Training Ship for Boys, Portsmouth 1862. She was sold for demolition in 1906 and broken up at Harvey's yard, Falmouth.

118. H.M.S. *St Vincent* arrived in Falmouth for breaking up on 23 June 1906 and interested visitors were charged a threepenny entrance fee in aid of Naval charities. Her six-ton Stock Anchor, manufactured in 1840, a unique example of Water Hammer Forging displayed for many years near Gyllyngvase, is now skilfully restored and graces the area ne the dockyard entrance.

. Holdroff's sail loft, Church Street, around the turn of the
tury has something of the air of an old wooden galleon which
yed off course up the slipway and stayed!

. Productivity, dexterity and industry in ship-shape Falmouth
ion in the light of Holdroff's sail loft at the turn of the
tury.

. *(overleaf)* Following their reception on the Moor, the
ice and Princess of Wales make their way to the ceremony of
laying of the foundation stone of Prince of Wales Pier in 1903.

122. The brave men of the Packet Service faced danger in the course of duty and Falmouth folk were proud of ther The granite obelisk on the Moor, dedicated to these fine men, was unveiled on 19 November 1898 with due respect and ceremony. The parade was led by the men of the *Ganges*.

123. The Proclamation of King George V was held on the Moor on 9 May 1910 and read out by the mayor. The impressive ceremony was attended by men of the Royal Garrison Artillery, Royal Engineers, the Navy and the Boys' Brigade, and watched by a crowd of thousands.

Hawker's damaged aeroplane
rd ship in Falmouth Harbour
nd 1925. The plane ditched
ie sea west of Ireland because
iel supply had run out. The
ship on the scene rescued the
and the second, with Charlie
vn (wearing cap) and 'Ferret'
ison, picked up the aircraft
proceeded to Falmouth. Young
ny Morrison was aboard (right).

125. The unusual structure known as The King's Pipe, next to the Custom House, was where contraband goods were burnt. It still operates today and when there is a good updraught it scatters ash and debris all along the street.

126. Falmouth Harbour Commissioners, founded in 1870, was brought into being as the harbour had been running unsuccessfully. The Killigrew's double-headed eagle and the anchor, introducing a nautical touch, were incorporated in the crest.

127. Dockyard workers in a mood of awe and excitement welcomed King George VI in May 1942 on a morale boosting visit to the Docks. The King was escorted by Chairman and owner H.A.J. 'Jack' Silley (left) with Ship Repa▮ General Manager Robert 'Bob' Smeaton from Gateshead on Tyne and Mr. Bartlett, General Manager, Falmouth Docks and Engineering Company.

128. Model yacht racing had long been a popular pastime in Falmouth and models were built with care and loving pride. Here we see the contestants for the model yacht racing regatta at Swanpool in 1906. Today, seafarers turn the hands to maritime model making, exact in every detail.

The nearer quay punt had adapted the spinnaker to suit the mast, which has had the head removed and spinnaker put on. These craft were 'bum boats' competing for the ship to shore trade with the merchant vessels; first on the was likely to secure a deal. Here they are racing in the 1895 Falmouth Regatta.

130.   The Vinnicombe family raced in regattas. Here we see *Boy Willie* cruising with the 'J' class yachts around 1920. Sadly, George Vinnicombe's father was taken ill in *Boy Willie* and died after being taken ashore at Cadgwith. Thus it was his last voyage; he died doing what he loved.

131. The Falmouth working/dredging boats traditionally raced. Here the old *Six Brothers*, skippered by George Vinnicombe, leads Toby West's *Victory* around the turning marker. Racing is taken very seriously and they are great rivals whilst it is all happening. Afterwards there is much yarning and jollification; friendships resume and rivalries are forgotten... until the next time!

132. The old *Six Brothers* 'hammering on' with George Vinnicombe at the helm. Built by 'Foreman' Ferris for Jimmy Lewarne, she was acquired by the Vinnicombes for oyster dredging. She was wrecked at Mylor in a severe south-easterly gale and a replica was built by Percy Dalton, the Penryn ship designer. Her shallow draught allowed her to drift over the oyster beds.

33. Bow on view of the Federal German Navy's three-masted barque *Gorch Fock*. On 25 July 1982, in perfect conditions under a clear blue sky, folk lined every hillside and took to the water in a variety of likely (and unlikely) craft to witness the spectacle of the Falmouth Tall Ships Race, an awe inspiring and unforgettable experience.

34. On board the *Gorch Fock* in Falmouth Harbour, July 1982.

135. The Polish barquentine *Pogoria*, another 'A' class contender, was easy to identify amidst the armada with her distinctively patterned sails. Everything went without a hitch, with Falmouth Harbour Master Captain David Banks responsible for their safe transit through the harbour. The Press launch, with the author and whisky-swigging journalists, escorted them off the Lizard.

136. Among all this ship-shape perfection of rigging and canvas is the cheeky, scruffy German brigantine *Outlaw*, seen in port the previous day with washing draped all over the place, dirty ropes, and great confusion. The authentic touch of a caged green parrot really captured the imagination.

137. At the age of 17 the Quaker lady Anna Maria Fox, one of the cultured and inventive Fox family who still live in Falmouth, was instrumental in forming the Polytechnic Society to 'Promote the useful and fine arts, to encourage industry and to elicit the ingenuity of a community distinguished for its mechanical skill'.

138. The Osborne family arrived in Falmouth at about the time of the railway, when Maurice Osborne's great-grandfather, a mason, was employed in the construction of the station. One of the Osbornes became a local schoolmaster, and Mr. E.A. Osborne, commonly known as 'Boss', founded the family photographic business which lasted 100 years until December 1984 when Maurice Osborne retired.

People

139. Marine artist Henry Scott Tuke (1858-1929) had a waterman's hut on
Custom House Quay, a specially adapted yacht with a large window set in the
gunwale, and a studio at Pennance Point. He instructed that his paintings
should be burnt on his death. Thus most of his best works were lost; the
remainder fetch high prices.

140. *(opposite above)* John West, 'Toby' West's grandad, had artistic talent and lived on a house boat near Submarine Pier. He was a protegé of the painter Tuke and specialised in marine subjects. He was said to be somewhat averse to small boys who happened to cross his bows.

141. *(opposite below left)* A local lad who made it to the top. Young Dennis Pascoe (second from right), the future Managing Director of Falmouth Docks, seen on a family sea-front stroll, sporting his Grammar School blazer at around the age of 13 in 1938. *Left to right*: Father, three friends, Mother, Dennis, sister. (His sister married an American Naval officer stationed at Falmouth.)

142. *(opposite below right)* Falmouth folk have a very high regard for Dennis Pascoe, who started work as a fitter apprentice in Falmouth Docks in September 1940. With his keen sense of humour and background of hard work and down to earth experience, he is regarded as something of a 'father' figure around Falmouth.

3. *(above)* 'Ferret' Morrison proudly displays his ʌyal Sturgeon on Fish Strand Quay. Traditionally every ʌrgeon caught has to be notified to the Monarch who s the first option. It was offered to the King, who was ʌring in Canada at the time, so instead of becoming ʌgly fare it was sold in Walter Morrison's wet fish shop 2s. 9d. per lb!

4. *(right)* Marine artist Tony Warren, who retains a ʌong visual boyhood memory of the war as seen on the ʌlmouth waterfront, takes a break from his studio. He ʌictured on Custom House Quay where pleasure craft ʌe taken the place of traditional trading vessels. ʌhind him is the steam tug *St Denys* (formerly the ʌrthgate Scott), which is part of Falmouth's Maritime ʌseum.

145. Vivian Pentecost, the future Coxswain of Falmouth Lifeboat, as he looked in 1937. He became one of the dare-devil Greenbank 'Water Rats' who demonstrated their prowess by swimming across to Flushing and back and who sometimes caused local boatmen to brandish their oars in frustration at their cheeky antics.

146. Over the years around Falmouth some things have not changed all that much. Having swapped one stylish outfit for another, completed an army caree and become Coxswain of the Falmouth Lifeboat, Vivian Pentecost is still smoking that pip

147. After a satisfying day's fishing George Vinnicombe (left), Robin, his younger brother and Clinton Powell proudly display their prize-winning catch of pollack.

148. 'Like father...like son...' Young Tim Vinnicombe carries on his family's traditions. Here he is seen emptying the dredge aboard the converted *Boy Willie*.

BIBLIOGRAPHY

Davidson, Robin, *Cornwall* (1978)

Dunston, Bob, *The Book of Falmouth and Penryn* (1975)

Farr, Grahame, *West Country Passenger Steamers* (1967)

Forestier-Walker, E. R., *Port of Enterprise* (1947)

Gay, Susan E., *Old Falmouth* (1903)

Greenhill, Basil, *The Merchant Schooners* (1951)

Mudd, David, *Home Along Falmouth and Penryn* (1980)

Murry, John, *A Handbook for Travellers in Devon and Cornwall* (1865)

Newman, Rodney, *The Charm of the Fal*

Noall, C. and Farr, G., *Wreck and Rescue Round the Cornish Coast* (1965)

Ward, C. S. and Baddeley, M. J. B., *Through Guides: South Devon and South Cornwall* (1895)

Whetter, James, *The History of Falmouth* (1981)